I0467779

Entrepreneur's Guide to Successful Sourcing

Josh Smith

Copyright © 2013 Josh Smith

Published by Shh Publishing at Smashwords

Prologue

Entrepreneurship is one of the most effective ways to build the life that you want to have. By establishing your own business you are in control of your earnings, the time you spend working and how your business is run. You are in charge of every controllable aspect of your life. Don't worry if you have to start out small. Just get started because you can build and expand as you go. Countless multi-million dollar empires began on a shoestring budget. The trick is to find the best suppliers of the products or services that you intend to market. Once you have a reliable product source at prices that allow you to compete in the market, develop your business plan and get the show on the road.

Building your basic business plan

When you are first starting a new business venture there are a few basic things that you will need to consider. In order to ensure your success, developing a business plan that outlines how you are going to start your business, what type of items you will sell, how you will sell them, start up capitol including a basic budget, and your short term goals will get you off to a good start.

Budgeting

The amount of start up funds you have to invest will determine your initial budget. Determine how much you will spend on the set up of your store front. If this is an online store, consider the cost of website operation, having your own domain and website hosting fees. Other items include costs of electronic payment processing and any fees that can be associated with it. For a bricks and mortar store front include space rental, utilities such as telephone, water, garbage, electricity and internet access. Other considerations may be shelving units to stock merchandise and office supplies. Don't forget to include a budget for advertising and marketing.

Product selection

Next, determine which products you will purchase to start out. There should be an assortment that includes variety of popular products that are appealing to your target audience of customers. By knowing what you are selling, you can develop a marketing plan for advertising the benefits and advantages of purchasing these products from you, to potential customers.

Volume and short term sales goals

By determining your sales goals you will have a rough estimate of how many items in each category you will need to stock for resale. This may also help you to plan on how often you'll need to reorder. It's important to make certain that you have an adequate supply to meet customer demands. It can take a while for new businesses to become established and well known by customers, so if your initial volume is less than you envisioned, you can make any needed adjustments as you go.

Develop a marketing plan to advertise your business

The first step in developing a marketing plan is to decide who your target audience will be. Based on the products that you are offering, are they male, female, both genders, young, old, etc. Once you have an idea of who is most apt to buy your merchandise you can set a strategy for reaching them. When you are trying to become established, marketing is not an area you want to skimp on. Fliers, brochures, business cards, newspaper and radio ads and internet advertising are good ways to gain exposure for your new business. If you include photos, make sure that they are detailed and professional looking. The first contact with your business sets the tone for how customers will perceive your operation. You want the first impression to be positive, interesting and inviting.

Next, it's time to find the best possible wholesale resources from which to purchase your inventory. Here are some tips to keep in mind as you browse through the large assortment of wholesalers that are vying for your attention.

What to Look for in a Supplier

The bottom line is that you are searching for a profit source for your business. Companies that understand this will offer high quality products, at reasonable prices, allowing retailers to make a tidy profit in sales. Quality wholesalers understand that when their customers are satisfied and are making good profits, it will result in repeat business for them. Read through the mission of the company in the about us section. This should give you an idea about the major goals of the company, and their policies towards customers. Here are some important qualities to look for in wholesale stores

1. High quality products that are guaranteed through a generous return policy

This helps to ensure that your business receives marketable products and does not get stuck with damaged goods that are a waste of time and money.

2. A broad variety of products to choose from that are appropriate for your business type

In order to make a profit you have to have an adequate supply of what customers want to purchase. Most people are looking for options such as different models, colors, etc.

3. Competitive pricing

You must be able to buy at prices that allow you to make a decent profit after all overhead expenses are satisfied.

4. Prompt shipping and order fulfillment

When you are depending on an order of goods to meet your sales goals and customer obligations, prompt shipping timelines are a must. In addition to this, getting the orders right the first time cuts down on time wasted on returns and reorders.

5. Excellent customer service help with easy methods of contact

We are all human, so on occasion, problems may arise even with the best companies. Customer service representatives that are easy to contact, and work fast to resolve any issues can make the difference between companies that are so so to deal with and those that provide excellence in service. Delays in problem resolution can translate into lost revenue for both you and the wholesaler. Prompt, friendly and professional attitudes are the things to look for in customer service communications.

The importance of establishing a good working relationship with your wholesale supplier

Your success may depend upon the quality of your relationship with your wholesale supplier. First and foremost, finding a high quality company that offers flexible terms and reliable support is the first priority. Not all wholesale companies are created equally. This often shows in the way their websites are laid out. If the site is hard to navigate and you cannot easily find the information that you are looking for, chances are that this lack of thoughtfulness towards customer comfort will transfer into the ways that they conduct their business transactions. It's best to go with what your gut feeling is telling you. First impressions count for very good reasons.

Companies that care about their customers will show it by making the best first impression possible. These are the businesses that you are more likely to have good working relationships with and it can make conducting business less frustrating and more profitable.

Find a company that caters to your unique business needs

Whether you are an established company, or starting out small, finding a wholesale store that is sensitive to your business needs is vital to the success of your venture. If you are just starting out and are working with a limited budget, there are wholesalers that are sensitive to this fact and have made provisions to help get you started. Here are some helpful policies that sensitive wholesale companies offer.

1. Waiver of EIN requirements

Businesses that are just starting out may begin as an individual testing the waters before applying for an EIN and formalizing the business. Wholesalers who are willing to give customers the same great prices without proof of a business license are contributing to the spirit of entrepreneurship and this form of encouragement can help new businesses to get their feet wet and wade in a little deeper on the next series of orders.

2. Multiple payment options

The facts are that many small businesses may get started with only one major credit card, or perhaps just a Paypal account. Wholesale stores that accept several different types of payment sources make it easier for new ventures to do business.

3. Smaller quantity offerings

When budget limitations are present, it is helpful to be able to order in smaller quantities and still get reasonable pricing that will allow for profit.

4. Clear policies on shipping costs

Ideally, the wholesaler you choose will combine shipping with the advertised price of the products being purchased. This is generally the case when free shipping policies are in force. This eliminates the surprise of getting your products to the checkout stage and discovering that the shipping costs make it more difficult for your business to make a profit.

Wholesale stores who offer these services are showing you that they want your business and will value you as a customer. You are more apt to have a smoother series of transactions and avoid the frustration of lost time and profits with stores that are sensitive to customer needs and requirements.

Ease of shopping by organizing categories

Wholesalers that provide neatly categorized items save shoppers time and effort by making it easy to locate the items that they are looking for. By placing them in categories that are accessible with a simple click of the mouse, customers are able to more quickly browse the selections that are available and begin adding to their shopping carts.

Some online wholesale stores place their items randomly on pages with no rhyme nor reason and it can take copious amounts of time to locate the items that customers are hoping to find. What is worse, is when there are no items of interest available and time has been spent on a search that yields no results.

Clear representation of available products

The presentation of the products available are important representations of the company's attention to details. This is an important aspect of how the company may work internally. When care is given to provide accurate and clear information, the rest of the services are more likely to be rendered in like fashion. In addition to organization by category, product descriptions that include a clear detailed photo of the item, followed by a name and description are important. Copious amounts of detail aren't necessary but

you need to know a little bit about what you are
considering for purchase.

Find a wholesale store that meets the demands of your customers

1. A variety of selections in product lines

Wholesale stores frequently make purchases from
liquidation sales and direct from manufacturers to deliver
the best possible prices for their customers. From time to
time new products are featured which may be appealing to
your customers. This can help boost your sales by adding
new or novel items that appeal to your customer base. Find
a wholesale store that offers a good selection in addition to
a variations in color and style of their products.

2. Consistent stock of the products you sell the most

In addition to adding new or novel items to your store, it is
of vital importance to maintain an adequate supply of the
products that your customers buy the most. Look at it this
way, when a customer begins to rely on your business for
finding a specific item, this sets you up for repeat business
and increased revenue. If you no longer offer the item that
they are accustomed to getting through you, they may
become disappointed and go to another retailer that is more
consistent in maintaining the supply. Choose a wholesale
store that maintains consistent supplies of the items that
your business requires.

3. High quality products

In order to keep your customers satisfied, you need to maintain a high standard for the type of items that you offer to the public. It is common sense that some inexpensive items are not made to last for long, such as disposable items made for single use. But there are some products that customers pay good money for and they expect to receive a value for their dollar. Look for companies that offer items that perform the way they are expected and hold up under normal use. The quality of the products that you sell will be a powerful determinant of repeat business and customer loyalty.

4. Clearly established policies

The best wholesale merchandise stores will have written policies that outline how their business transactions with you will be conducted. For example, shipping policies should give information about the timelines involved, the methods or shipping providers which are used, how much shipping will cost, and what the company's policy states about lost, delayed, damaged or incorrect orders. The best companies will work with customers on an individual basis to ensure that they are highly satisfied with the goods and services, and that every reasonable effort is made to ensure prompt and accurate delivery of goods promised.

5. A statement of the mission of the company

The company's mission statement should be displayed prominently or at least easy to access with a brief search. These are generally located in the about us section for online stores. By sharing the overall goals of the company, readers can gain a sense of how they may be treated as customers. When companies do not share their philosophy on customer service, it could mean that this is not a top priority. As a new business owner you have the right and the responsibility to be selective about the companies that you are willing to do business with. Your bottom line may depend upon this.

The value of mission statements

This point cannot be overemphasized when you are looking for a good company to deal with. When a company establishes a mission statement and makes it readily available for potential customers, it makes a powerful statement about how the company is most likely to function internally. Mission statements establish the philosophy by which the organization is managed and operated. This is the key component that is used to bring all of the team members together as a working unit. It inspires workers to put customer service as a top priority, and in turn, to perform their duties to the best of their abilities. To sum it up, you are more likely to receive top quality services from these companies.

Considerations for establishing a working relationship with your wholesale supplier

If you have found a company that you believe meets the criteria you have established for meeting your business needs, it's wise to set up an account with the company and start doing business on a small scale. If you have questions that have not been answered through the website (there shouldn't be too many), then send an email through their contact us section. The response that you receive will help you to assess how quickly their customer service reps respond to customer queries, their level of helpfulness and professionalism, and if they are a company that will be responsive to your needs.

The ordering and payment portions of your experience should be seamless for the most part. Product location and cart additions should flow smoothly. Checkout may require some additional information and options for payment and delivery, but this is fairly standard. You want your wholesaler to gather enough information so they can do the best job possible. Even if it takes a little more time to complete.

Once your order is placed and delivered, you will get an idea about the reliability of the company. If the ordering, payment and delivery of goods processes all run smoothly, you have most likely found a company that will be a reliable source of product acquisitions.

What to avoid when searching for wholesale companies

While it may sound petty to include the negative things to look for, as an entrepreneur, you owe it to the success of your business to stay informed on what to avoid as well as what to look for in wholesale companies.

1. A disorganized appearance on the website.

Your initial impression is most likely the best guide for judging the integrity of a company. A sloppy or disorganized site may be an indication of the way that the company is operated. This is foretelling of the quality of service you may receive. If the products are displayed in a disorganized fashion that makes finding specific items difficult to find, this is a bad sign. Companies that pay attention to important details will make it easy to find what you're looking for.

2. Difficulty in finding contact information

When it is hard to locate a reliable way to contact a company about questions you may have, it can appear that they are discouraging this type of activity. Customer service is not shown to be a high priority or there would be clear pathways to the appropriate links. It could be that this aspect of the website design was just not well thought out. But if this is the case, there may be other important things that are poorly planned or disregarded.

3. Poor communications

If you send an inquiry through a company's contact us link and you receive a slow, or no response at all, this is a red flag that indicates that customers are not their top priority. These are companies that should be avoided as it may be impossible to establish a healthy business relationship with them. Communication is key in problem solving when issues arise. It can end up costing you time and money. Often, time spent trying to resolve issues does translate into lost money.

4. Inflexible terms for new customers

Wholesale companies that are interested in meeting customer needs will try to adapt to all potential customers. This includes small businesses that may have limited choices for payment methods and the need to order in smaller quantities. Companies that only sell to established businesses with EINs and require that large bulk orders be paid with a limited amount of payment options are going for the big bucks and come across as being unresponsive to the needs of small businesses. If you are just getting started and cannot move a large volume of goods, these companies are not suited for your requirements.

5. Inconsistent inventory supplies

Wholesale companies that frequently run out of stock for items that you need a consistent supply of may not be the best choice for you. While popular items may tend to be sold out frequently, companies that do not maintain a consistent availability of the majority of products you purchase on a regular basis can end up costing you business and damage your reputation for meeting customer expectations.

6. Stringent policies that are not customer oriented

While the best online wholesale companies maintain policies that protect the interest of the customer, there are others who are fond of using disclaimers to cover any mistakes that are made. If a company does not offer plainly worded policies on ordering, customer satisfaction, order fulfillment and shipping processes, you have no reason to feel secure in ordering from them. You have the right and the responsibility to ensure that the company you are dealing with will deliver prompt and accurate services. It's best to avoid the shop at your own risk scenario when spending your business capital.

7. Frequent late deliveries

When a company gives estimates on delivery times, you can expect a few days leeway one way or the other. When late deliveries become a problem for your business it is time to look for a different vendor. Some things that you should be mindful of are the amount of time that it takes the company to fulfill the order and whether or not they are shipping them out by the promised deadlines. Keeping promises is an important part of maintaining professional integrity. When the orders are in transit, the company is no longer responsible, what matters is that they make the effort to ensure that orders are shipped out as promised.

8. Issues with order fulfillment

Consistent mistakes in order fulfillment can become time consuming and expensive. When companies ship out the wrong items to your business, it could mean that your customers will not be able to find the items that they are looking for through your business. This can translate into losing customers and a decrease in revenue.

9. Lack of responsiveness for problem resolution

If a wholesale company does not respond in a timely and professional manner to issues that may arise in the transactions that you are completing with them, this signals the potential for poor attitudes towards customer satisfaction. The best companies will place responsiveness to customers as a high priority.

The reasons that you may want to avoid companies that meet the above criteria are not personal, they relate solely to your satisfaction and safety in conducting business with high quality and caring companies that will value your patronage. Any departures from providing excellence in customer service and accurate and prompt services are indicators that you could find better companies to do business with. Large time spent trying to resolve issues can cost your company in customer attrition and lost revenues.

In Conclusion

Entrepreneurship is one of the most exciting ventures that an individual can embark upon. Although it can seem a bit daunting if this is your first experience, the rewards can be immensely satisfying. The tips provided in this article are meant to help you start out on the right foot to get your new business on track from day one. By learning how to develop your business plan, and set a few short term goals, you can be on your way to the start of a new life and career.

Deciding what products you will offer, how you will sell them and what it will take to get started is the first step. After this, you'll set up a budget so you will know how much capitol you will need to start. When you've set your budget in place you're ready to move forward. Determining your target audience and finding ways to advertise your business to them is the next. When this is done it's time to find your supplier and start stocking your shelves.

There are hundreds of wholesale stores and suppliers to choose from and this is one of the reasons we've provided you with some tips on what to look for and what to avoid when choosing a company to deal with. Not all wholesale stores are created equal. There are companies that strive to meet the needs of their customers with flexible policies that help new businesses to become established without a hassle or large amounts of red tape to wade through. These are the companies that you will find are most likely to help you turn a decent profit. Since making a profit is the bottom line for new businesses, there is a need for you to be aware of what makes a wholesale supplier the best choice. This gives your new venture a better chance of growing and thriving at a faster pace.

Wholesale companies that offer opportunities for small businesses or even individual entrepreneurs to start out small and expand, stand as excellent models for businesses to emulate. By reading the mission statement of the company, you should be able to gain a sense of how they conduct business throughout the organization. This often translates into superior customer service and accuracy in all of their dealings. Companies that pay attention to detail and provide websites that are well organized and easy to navigate have done their homework and send the message that they value their customers.

By following the tips that we've provided, you have a solid foundation of knowledge that will help you get your new business off on the right foot. Information is the key to making sound business decisions. Any entrepreneur who has achieved a level of success can agree to this. We hope that the information provided will help to to make the best possible choices that will give your new business venture the best possible start.

About the Author

Josh Smith is an internet retailer who specializes in Retail Arbitrage. He has successfully started his own business from the ground up with Retail Arbitrage and currently is helping others do the same..

Remember to take action!

Without action, there is no success.

Success is the continuation of a worthy ideal.

Connect with the author at info@retailarbitrage.org

Other books by This Author

Please visit your favorite Ebook retailer to discover other books by Josh Smith!

Retail Arbitrage

www.ingramcontent.com/pod-product-compliance
Lightning Source LLC
Chambersburg PA
CBHW041617180526
45159CB00002BC/895